Contents

My name is Anne.

I am going to play **baseball**!

5

I am a **catcher**.

I wear **pads** and a **face mask**.

They will keep me safe.

I sit behind the **batter**.

The batter tries to hit the balls that the **pitcher** throws to me.

I catch the balls that the batter does not hit.

I catch the balls in my **glove**.

11

I take off my pads and face mask when it is my team's turn to bat.

13

Now, I will bat.

I put on my **batting helmet**.

15

The pitcher throws the ball.

I swing the bat.

I hit the ball hard!

17

The ball goes far.

An **outfielder** picks it up.

19

Playing baseball is fun!

21

New Words

baseball (**bayss**-bawl) a game played with a bat and a ball on a field with four bases; there are two teams of nine players each

batter (**bat**-ur) the player who tries to hit the ball thrown by the pitcher

batting helmet (**bat**-ing **hel**-mit) a covering to protect the batter's head

catcher (**ka**-chur) the player who catches balls that are not hit by the batter

face mask (**fayss mask**) a covering to protect the catcher's face

glove (**gluhv**) a padded covering for the hand

outfielder (**out**-feel-dur) a player who stays in the outfield

pads (**padz**) pieces of soft material, such as cotton or foam rubber, used for protection

22

pitcher (**pich**-ur) the player who throws the ball

To Find Out More

Books
Baseball ABC
by Florence Cassen Mayers
Harry N. Abrams

My Baseball Book
by Gail Gibbons
William Morrow & Company

Web Site
Kid's Domain Baseball Fun
http://www.kidsdomain.com/sports/baseball
Learn baseball trivia, play online games, and do a word scramble on this fun Web site.

Index

About the Author

Edana Eckart has written several children's books. She enjoys bike riding with her family.

Reading Consultants

Kris Flynn, Coordinator, Small School District Literacy, The San Diego County Office of Education

Shelly Forys, Certified Reading Recovery Specialist, W.J. Zahnow Elementary School, Waterloo, IL

Sue McAdams, Former President of the North Texas Reading Council of the IRA, and Early Literacy Consultant, Dallas, TX